Our Highest Calling

The Study Guide

Welcoming Others to Christ

through Discipleship

in Love

Sang W. Sur, Ph.D., Th.D.

© 2020 Sang Sur

Published by Prayer Tents Media
Old Tappan, NJ

All rights reserved. No portion of this book may be reproduced, stored in a retrieval system, or transmitted in any form or by any means—electronic, mechanical, photocopy, recording, scanning, or other—except brief quotations in critical reviews or articles, without the prior written permission of the publisher.

Scripture quotations are taken from the Holy Bible, New Living Translation, copyright © 1996, 2004, 2015 by Tyndale House Foundation. Used by permission of Tyndale House Publishers, a Division of Tyndale House Ministries, Carol Stream, Illinois 60188. All rights reserved.

Our Highest Calling
ISBN 978-1-953167-00-2 (Hardcover, English)
ISBN 978-1-953167-07-1 (Softcover, English)
ISBN 978-1-953167-02-6 (Kindle e-book, English)
ISBN 978-1-953167-04-0 (Other e-book, English)
ISBN 978-1-953167-03-3 (Hardcover, Korean)
ISBN 978-1-953167-08-8 (Softcover, Korean)
ISBN 978-1-953167-09-5 (Other e-book, Korean)
ISBN: 978-1-953167-20-0 (Hardcover, Spanish)
ISBN: 978-1-953167-21-7 (Other e-book, Spanish)

The Study Guide:
ISBN 978-1-953167-18-7 (Study Guide, English)
ISBN 978-1-953167-19-4 (Study Guide, Korean)

Library of Congress Control Number: 2020942011

Contents

Getting Started 1

Chapter 1. The Great Commission 3

    The Great Commission does not tell us to evangelize. It tells us to make disciples. 3

    Matthew 28:19-20 Has Five Key Commands or Callings 3

Chapter 2. The Good News Explained 6

    Faith Comes from God 7

    Problem with Past Tactics to Build Metrics of Number of People Saved: 7

    Relationships Are Required to Teach People What It Means to be in a Relationship with God 8

    Contextualize and Be Where People Are 8

Chapter 3: How Jesus and His Disciples Made Other Disciples 9

    Disciples of Jesus Were People Who Had Interest in God 9

    How did Jesus Actually Make People into Disciples? 9

    Key Points of Acts 2:42-47 13

    The Original Understanding of the Gospel Message 14

    Development of the Catholic Church 17

    Salvation by Works Protested – The Protestant Reformation 18

    Period of Enlightenment (18th century) 18

    Industrial Revolution (18-19th century) 19

    Availability of Education for the Wealthy, the Increase in Gap Between Those Who Have and Do Not 19

    Internet and Availability of Education; Individualism (Today) 20

    Class Meetings – John Wesley's Attempt to Restore Discipleship 20

Chapter 5. Effective Strategies for Evangelism. 22

    How Should Christians Live, and How Can We Fulfill the Great Commission? 22

    Passionate Prayer Meetings in Small Groups That Changed the World 22

    Contextualization 23

    Business as a Mission 24

Theology of Contextualization 25

Development of Interest-based Small Groups 26

Chapter 6. Our Highest Calling is Love 28

Recap of Chapter 2 – the Gospel, Where the Purpose is to Restore the Relationship with God 28

Modern Day Small Groups That Do Not Practice Relationships 29

A True Small Group Supports One Another to Look Up Together 29

Sharing Lives is the Priority of Small Groups. 29

Our Highest Calling (2 Peter 1:5-9) 31

God is Love (1John 4:7-8) 34

Love in Practice (1Corinthians 13) 36

Chapter 7. Being a Disciple to Make Disciples 38

Small Groups Have Two-Fold Purpose 38

Basic Structures of a Small Group 38

Results of Each Gathering 39

Components of a Small Group (Acts 2:42) 39

Meeting Location 39

Characteristics of Strong Small Groups 39

Possible Content for Small Group Meetings 39

Eat Together! (Eating Ministry) 40

Power Evangelism 40

Proper Length of Small Group Meetings 40

Special Small Group – Families 40

Number of Small Groups to Join 40

When Should I Start a Small Group? 40

When Should We Disband? 40

When and How Should We Split? 40

What a Small Group is Not 41

How to Evangelize 41

Role of Pastors in Small Groups 41

Goal of Every Meeting 41

Getting Started

> **❝** *Love has always been the highest calling;*
> *Don't substitute it for anything less. (p. 113)*

God has called us to more than attending services and living a good moral life. He has called us to be like Him, who is love. The Church is called to demonstrate Him in our daily living, but the Church is often not where either Christians and those who do not yet believe associate with love.

Jesus calls us to a relationship with God. Through this study, I hope that we look at relationships with one another differently as it likely resembles your relationship with God.

As such, studying the book on your own may be beneficial, especially if you intend to lead a study on it; but I encourage you to gather with other believers who desire to grow in their relationship with God to reflect together on the contents outlined in the book.

In many ways, this book is an incomplete product dependent on Christians like you to fulfill the message of the Scriptures. Loving others is not something anyone can teach but can only be modeled and aspired after, especially as the Holy Spirit enables you to do so. So as you study this book, ask the Holy Spirit to lead and guide you in the way you think and live out your life. Remember, God has done great things through a small group of people who gathered together to pray. Your study may be the beginning of that great start.

In Christ's Love,

Sang Sur

Practical Guidance.

- If possible, read through the book before covering chapters in this study guide. When your group gathers together, read through the drop quotes to refresh your memory of the chapter's crucial points.

- Spend more time dialoguing with one another about matters of life. It is ok not to be able to complete the entire chapter in one sitting. However, it is essential to go deep and share lives together and commit to one another on how you should live as a result of the discussion.

- Trust God to lead your study. The book or this study does not transform you. God can. Allow Him to speak and allow for opportunities to pray together as you go through the study.

- Spend more time on listening to thoughts of others in the group discussions and end of chapter reflections.

- Enjoy time with one another. Enjoy your time with God together.

Chapter 1. The Great Commission

Group Reflections.

How do you evangelize? Or when you think about evangelism, what are the activities that come to mind?

The Great Commission does not tell us to evangelize. It tells us to make disciples.

- **Evangelism**: Bringing the Good News and sharing what it means to neighbors who do not know Christ.
- **Missions**: Making disciples of Jesus where local bodies of Christ do not exist by sending or being sent
- **Discipleship**: Living a lifestyle of spending time with others, or living life together

All three work together in both the local and global call directed to *all Christians*. They are not something only pastors do.

The Great Commission does not say to "go forth" or "evangelize." Going forth means to start something new, but Jesus called us to *live it out continually*. It also does not say *just to share* what the Good News is. He said to *make disciples* by going, baptizing, and teaching.

Evangelism may be associated with teaching, and teaching can be done online with modern technology. Yet, there is a reason we must go and live amongst people who do not believe in Jesus: the ability to believe requires time, and it requires others in community. *Discipleship forms that community where people can come to faith over time.*

Discipleship includes learning life from another, to become like that person

Matthew 28:19-20 Has Five Key Commands or Callings

- *All believers* are to work together to fulfill this call

- - This call is not for individuals, such as pastors, but for all believers to work together to fulfill the call in communion.
- Go after those who do not know God
  - Form a place where people who have not grown up in a Christian environment to come to know God over time
- Make disciples as we are going, baptizing, and teaching
  - Continual (going) life-on-life relationships that include baptizing and teaching along the way.
  - Baptism is a public declaration of faith
  - Teaching means life-value sharing with hands-on training like learning an instrument. It requires interaction.
  - Discipleship involves life-on-life living together – that is, "near and working together over time."
  - Discipleship environment: 1) provides a comfortable setting for learning, 2) enables people to be who they are, 3) allows observation of other believers, 4) welcomes asking questions
- Guard our faith and pass it along
  - Τηρέω (tireo) = keep firm and guard. Preserve what God has taught us, and pass the learnings along
  - Implications to be a good role model for another to follow → discipleship
- Trust in God
  - Μετά (meta) = "in the midst of" or "together with."
  - Trust that God is there, and take risks as God calls
  - Jesus protects and empowers us by sending us the Holy Spirit. He will be with us always, even to the end of the age.

> 66 *Busy people cannot be available. Busy people cannot love in action.* (p. 23)

Chapter Reflections.
1. What does discipleship mean to you? Share an experience of discipleship you had and try to correlate it to the learnings from this chapter.
2. What are some changes you may need to make in your life in order to make disciples as Jesus commands?

Chapter 2. The Good News Explained

> **❝** *The reason Jesus died was to bridge the broken relationship. (p. 28)*

Many people believe the Gospel partially, and that causes them to be stuck in religion. Consider the wrong understanding of the Gospel.

The wrong way:

> *Since people were sinful, Jesus died to forgive us of our sins. We just need to repent of our sins and we would be forgiven.*

Though the above is Biblical and true, it is only the partial message of the Good News that Jesus brings. It is focused on the wrong object.

The correct way:

> *God wanted a relationship with us. To enable the relationship, Jesus died to be the perfect sacrifice. Now, we can walk with Him.*

This is the complete Gospel. It begins from the creation story in Genesis to Jesus's death to remove the problem of sin to the pouring of the Holy Spirit so that we may walk with Him.

The Gospel is about a *relationship with God*. The focus is not on the *forgiveness of sin*. Consider the ramification of misunderstanding the purpose of the Gospel:

Focus on relationship	Focus on forgiveness of sin
Walking with God leading to constant dependence and conversations with God	Continual Repentance leading to reduced/no honest conversation with God
Recognizes imperfections, but also acceptance	Distancing from God with desire to hide
Relationship takes priority. Not accomplishing is ok	Sacrifice takes priority, which means need to work harder and be better

Sonship – learn to be a child of God	Feelings of apathy, failure, guilt, and not measuring up
Trusts God the Father to breakthrough and provide	Feels the person was not repentant enough and worries. Less/no faith to take action
Leads to a relationship	Leads to religion (as is true in many churches)

Group Reflections.
1. Describe the Gospel in your own words.
2. Do you find your understanding of the Gospel to be more relationship focused or sin focused?

Faith Comes from God

- Salvation is a gift from God. It is not something people make a decision out of their own will.

Problem with Past Tactics to Build Metrics of Number of People Saved

- We cannot know if a person has come to faith other than through personal testimony, which ought to lead to baptism
- Reading specified prayers (such as "sinners prayer") does not make the person a Christian. Such methods are focused on the times the Christian is doing the evangelistic efforts, yet God's timing is not something for us to control. **God provides the faith.** It is not for us to determine.
    - Altar calls, mourners bench, "sinner's prayer" may lead people to false faith and nominal Christianity. Even Christians with titles in churches may not be saved.
- Christians can only allow time to welcome and provide an atmosphere of love for the interested person and allow God to work on His own time

Relationships Are Required to Teach People What It Means to be in a Relationship with God

- Modern problems: busyness of Christians.
- Rather life-modeling through close proximity over time is required

Contextualize and Be Where People Are

- Apostle Paul – I lived like, have become, I too lived, When I am with… they show that Paul worked hard to fit in with others so that he may have opportunities to share the Gospel in a way they can understand.
- Christians must learn to share their lives with interested people so that they may come to know Christ.

Group Reflections.
How can you share lives with interested people?

Chapter Reflections.
1. How does the gospel, the Good News of Jesus Christ, affect your everyday living?
2. How is your relationship with Jesus? How goes your soul?

Chapter 3: How Jesus and His Disciples Made Other Disciples

Jesus demonstrated how to make disciples through His ministry.

Disciples of Jesus Were People Who Had Interest in God

- Matthew 4:18-22 – Simon Peter, Andrew, James, and John dropped whatever they were doing when Jesus called them. They were looking for something more.
- God initiates that interest
- Many young people today are seeking the same

Disciples of Jesus were regular men. No one of great stature.

Jesus's disciples eventually made other disciples and have formed what is called the Church today.

How did Jesus Actually Make People into Disciples?

By:

- Walking with them
- Showing them
- Teaching them hand-in-hand

Examples:

- Jesus exemplified teaching to the crowds. Disciples probably ate with Jesus, asked questions, and had other insights that they can only receive by being in close proximity with Him.
- Jesus exemplified life of miracles while teaching that it occurs by faith
- Jesus taught them about the costs of placing faith in God
- Jesus taught them to persevere in faith, especially against leaders who understood or taught about God incorrectly
- Jesus taught to center on God and not the demands of the crowd
- Jesus taught to share stories
- Jesus taught that God is more interested in the heart than what we do

Group Reflections.
1. Describe how Jesus's way of discipleship differs from today's church settings.
2. In your current context, how can discipleship look like?

How Jesus's Disciples Did Discipleship

The apostles were responsible for discipling thousands-upon-thousands of people coming to faith in God.

- Sudden growth of small groups as shown in Acts 2:42-47 probably occurred due to instructions from the apostles. It focused on (verse 42):
    - Learning about God
    - Sharing lives together
    - Eating together, and
    - Prayer

- Reasons why the first Church were collection of small groups:
    - Shared lives together (fellowship) and ate together, which *cannot be done within a crowd.*
    - Shared belongings with others, which *cannot be done within a crowd.*
    - Ability to dialogue at a personal level to determine needs of others, which *cannot be done within a crowd.*
    - Meeting at temple courts points to gathering of many small groups. Verse 46 says the same people also met in their homes and ate together, which *cannot be done within a crowd.*

- Discipleship are person-to-person, life-on-life connections. Christians who have a relationship with God can share the same with those who are interested in God. Others can see and experience God through such relationships

- Modern churches do not have the same infrastructure as the first Church

- A place where people can individually grow from *where they are* and *along the way*.

Group Reflections.
1. What are some existing gatherings where people can individually grow from where they are and along the way?
2. If you were to plant a new church, how would you implement such infrastructures where people can individually grow from where they are and along the way?

Christians Are Not Saviors!

- It is God's prerogative to bring about salvation. He provides the faith.
- Evangelizing at locations and at times when convenient to the believer does not bring about faith
- Christians can simply welcome them to relationships that exist over time.
- Christians can pray for the people who are interested in God.
    - Intercede, seek God's will, communicate what God is saying to them. God may respond and provide tangible relief to the not-yet-believer

Group Reflections.
What are ways you can welcome people who may be interested in God to relationships that persists over time?

Chapter Reflections.
1. How do you practice discipleship?
2. How do people around you know that you are a disciple of Jesus?

Chapter 4. History of the Gospel, Evangelism, and Missions

Remember Christ's disciples. They rowed their heavy ships to shore, then abandoned everything to follow Christ.

—Elfric of Eynsham

> ❝ The history will show how Christianity has now become a passive religion to many people and will emphasize the need for a reform—a return to discipleship—that will bring us back to the gospel that Jesus taught. (p. 54)

First churches formed out of gatherings of small groups. We get a glimpse of what small groups looked like from Acts 2:42-47:

> *42 All the believers devoted themselves to the apostles' teaching, and to fellowship, and to sharing in meals (including the Lord's Supper), and to prayer. 43 A deep sense of awe came over them all, and the apostles performed many miraculous signs and wonders. 44 And all the believers met together in one place and shared everything they had. 45 They sold their property and possessions and shared the money with those in need. 46 They worshiped together at the Temple each day, met in homes for the Lord's Supper, and shared their meals with great joy and generosity. 47 all the while praising God and enjoying the goodwill of all the people. And each day the Lord added to their fellowship those who were being saved.*
>
> *Acts 2:42-47 (NLT)*

Key Points of Acts 2:42-47

- The purpose of their coming together as a small group was for four things (v. 42):
    - Apostle's teaching (study and learn Scriptures together, to explore what God wants them to know, knowledge)
    - Fellowship (relationships, getting to know each other at an intimate level, love for one another)
    - Eating together (recognizing that no one is better than the other and are the same, recognize that they are one in Christ [Lord's Supper])

- - Prayer (trust in God together, both individually and collectively. Lay down priorities and allow God to lead)
- Met/gathered together in one place and they were all one (common, not different from one another) (verse 44).
- (Only available in small groups) people sold their properties and possessions to share with anyone in need. (verse 45)
  - This may have been a characteristic when a small group had some members who had more needs than the other. Luke would not have emphasized this unless this characteristic was important.
  - People knew each other intimately, and they gave out of that relationship
    - Today, not many church members know each other, but they feel entitled to borrow money from other believers because "Christians are supposed to give"
- The small group worshipped God together by the temple courtyard (verse 46)
  - Picture of mass worship. The key difference: Instead of bunch of strangers, there were groups of people that knew each other intimately. Their worship likely involved conversations, asking questions, and worshipping with all their heart and love (as would be recognized by one another within their small groups)
- They met in their homes to eat together (verse 46)
- More people continued to come to these gatherings (verse 47).

New disciples were made this way, in ways where lives are shared. This was the understanding of the Great Commission back in those days.

The Original Understanding of the Gospel Message

- (From Chapter 2) Focus on relationships. Why? People recognized their relationship to one another was a correlation to their relationship with God. (For example, when people give to others in need, they recognize they were giving to God, Matthew 25:40, 45)
- How can people have a deep relationship with God? By their faith in God, which is enabled by the grace of God.
- *It is through personal and deep fellowship with one another while seeking God together that the Church grew in numbers and in hearts.*

Remember, Jesus rebuked the Pharisees for enforcing laws, but not focusing on the heart. It was an individualistic set of rules that the people must keep to be in good standing. Jesus focused on relationships, or the heart. Small groups recognized this.

Group Reflections.
1. How do modern-day churches reflect the first churches? Describe its impacts and implications.
2. Do you feel the churches today are rule-based or focused on relationships? Explain your views.

In 325 AD. – Constantine nationalized the Church as the official religion of Rome. Though it sounds good that a nation can turn to God, it created "Christians" who did not truly believe but acted in the ways (laws) as defined by the government. This led them back to the reasons why Jesus rebuked the Pharisees! Other impacts:

- Separation of title (Elite versus the common)
- No more testimonies
- Religious activities as defined by the Church, not from the heart
- Less dependence on the Holy Spirit, but uniformity of knowledge

Church established by Jesus and His disciples	Church after 325 AD	Church today
Anyone can share about their experiences with God including miracles and God's provision	Must hear the "truth" from the clergy	?
Anyone can share about their lives and experiences. Those who have walked with God can guide the members to walk a life of faith.	Only the educated people can share the right way to live. Others (common people) must listen and accept.	?
Living by faith is encouraged in every day living by direct example and practice.	"Christians" must do whatever is dictated to them.	?
Christians relied on the Holy Spirit to lead them. No small group was alike, and life was shared differently among them.	Knowledge about God becomes catholic (uniform), and clergy knows exactly what to do.	?
People experience miracles and supernatural provision.	Christians had the same common experience of God	?

Group Reflections.
Fill in the question marks above. Share the implications of your responses.

Some spin offs

- Asceticism: to separate oneself from society because they recognized the rigidity of the national religion. They became like hermits who tried to live out their lives in isolation from the world.
    o Though intentions may be good, Jesus did not call His people to be outside the world. Christians are to be a living influence in the world, though they are not of it.

Development of the Catholic Church

- Pope and bishops claimed authority to tell laypersons if and how their sins can be forgiven. If the person did not follow their direction, they would not be allowed to take part in the eucharistic communion. Penance laws were established and penitentials were compiled. A person would be forgiven of their sins by following the specific direction of the pope and bishops.
    - Truth: Forgiveness of sin belongs to Jesus. We just need to confess our sins to Him, and because of what Jesus has done for us on the cross, we are forgiven (1John 1:9). This is the difference between law that leads to sacrifices (doing) versus the transformation of the heart (recognition that only God can save, and coming before God)
- Concept of penance continued to develop toward forgiveness by works, and even to forgiveness to those who can afford it – the wealthy
    - Can be forgiven for committed sins, or even sins in advance
    - Extra-biblical concept of purgatory, a place where people heading to heaven must be purified of their temporal sins. Indulgences can reduce the time and severity of the purification. For higher cost, temporal sins can be completely forgiven.
    - Crusades, people can be completely forgiven when they join a war. Their heart no longer matters, a relationship with God does not exist, they just need to perform some works to have eternal life.
    - When church needed money, they hired professional quaestores (pardoners) to gather funds for specific projects. Rouen Cathedral in France today is known as the "butter tower" because it was built by funds raised from selling indulgences.

Group Reflections.
Did the people in the times of the Catholic Church rule recognize that they had the wrong faith? Consider this from the perspectives of the common person, the government, and from the leadership of the Church.

Salvation by Works Protested – The Protestant Reformation

- A priest named Martin Luther could not correlate the practice of salvation by works when Scriptures said salvation is through faith.

Period of Enlightenment (18th century)

- Advent of sciences leads theology to be another field of study. Understanding of God becomes purely educational and academic for clergy. Less about the heart, more about the head.
- Miracles and Supernatural provisions of God are discounted as it does not fit the logic of the sciences.
- Worship services are less about God, but a place to fill our knowledge.

Group Reflections.
Is your understanding of God more from the head or the heart?
In your culture, do you highly value education and knowledge?
How could that impact your relationship with God?

Industrial Revolution (18-19th century)

- Specialized jobs. Taking a role of a clergy was no longer a calling, but another profession like a lawyer, an accountant, or an engineer. Educated people do one thing well, which was not the case in the past.

Group Reflections.
How are you specialized? Could this limit you from fulfilling the purposes God has for your life?

Availability of Education for the Wealthy, the Increase in Gap Between Those Who Have and Do Not

- Sunday School is an example of how even the Church distinguished the wealthy and the common people. Sunday School is a concept where the educated people can teach the uneducated. Wealthy people took on that role, bringing back teachings by the few, and not by all believers.

Internet and Availability of Education; Individualism (Today)

- Individualism says one must keep on excelling on their own, as opposed to priority of the kingdom of God first. The Bible never promoted this, but with increase in specializations of work, even believers today consider themselves faithful when they do their work well, while the pastor does his/her "work" well.
- Specialized/professional sermon speakers are readily available on the web. They provide good amount of knowledge. People flock to such and consider filling of their knowledge as a time of worship.
  - Did you know, in most denominations, sermons, benedictions, baptisms, the Lord's supper, and even prayers for miracles and healings are solely given and administered by ordained pastors? Is this a cultural influence or something that is prescribed in the Bible?
- It is no longer about gathering, relationships, and love for one another (and therefore about God), but about growing in knowledge to be better on their own.

The fact that we emphasize the need for knowledge shows that we follow the culture. What should take greater priority?

Group Reflections.
How accurate or inaccurate is the picture of today's church? How is today's church different compared to that of discipleship that Jesus and his disciples taught and practiced?

Class Meetings – John Wesley's Attempt to Restore Discipleship

- How is it with your soul? How is your relationship with God today?
- This question led to an accountability to the way they lived.
- Met weekly, and attendance was a requirement (missing one or two may be acceptable with reason, but not tolerated)

Group Reflections.
How does your or a typical Christian's everyday life reflect their faith today?

Chapter Reflections
1. How does your current practice of worship and discipleship match up with what is prescribed in the Scriptures?
2. What do you believe to be your great calling of God? How can you ensure that it is purely from God and is not tainted by the cultural norms and trends?

Chapter 5. Effective Strategies for Evangelism.

How Should Christians Live, and How Can We Fulfill the Great Commission?

- Every Christian is a missionary, a person who is called to make disciples (Matthew 28:19-20)
- Making disciples is done by building relationship with the few.
- Evangelism occurs in a community of love, and that is what it means to make disciples.

> 66 *Especially in many churches today, it is normal for the members to only see each other once a week. There is no accountability, no prayer for one another, and ultimately, no growth. In a culture where individualism is encouraged, this is the norm. (p. 77)*

Yet, today's trend of individualism leads to isolation and hiding of our true selves. The cultural example of this is shown in concepts of dating and interviews.

Passionate Prayer Meetings in Small Groups That Changed the World

- Early movements of the Protestant Reformation recognized importance of small groups. Specifically, that in order to grow in intimacy with God, small groups of people who loved one another dedicated to study the Scriptures, pray together, and live out authentic Christian lives were necessary.
- 1714, Count Nicholaus Ludwig von Zinzendorf, at age 14, formed the "Ordered of the Grain of Mustard Seed." With five other boys, they dedicated to pray together to give witness to the power of Jesus Christ. When Zinzendorf was 22, Moravians came to his house asking for help. By age of 32, he funded the first two Moravian missions, which is the precursor to worldwide missions movement today.

- - Zinzendorf and Moravians both lived out lives within small groups where they met often to follows spiritual disciplines and encourage one another
  - William Carey wrote a book on around the year 1800 that talked about mission societies whose purposes are to take the Gospel to the unreached world. His writing led to the modern Protestant missionary movement that were followed on by many others. His book and his practices are the precursor to modern missionary movements such as YWAM, CRU, and many others.

Modalities and Sodalities

- Modality – mainstream church – a structured fellowship with minimal limitation to join
- Sodality – Mission organizations - a structured fellowship that requires a commitment and has bars to entry
- Example of membership in a town (modality) vs running a small business in the town (sodality)

Yet, both sodalities and modalities are equally important. Sodalities are not para-church, as to mean they are inferior to the mainstream church. They complement each other, and both are necessary.

Sodalities reach specific people and lead to person-to-person discipleship. It additionally welcomes not-yet-Christians to dialogue. This is where contextualization comes into play.

Contextualization

Does everyone need to worship God the same way you do?

Failed Missions: United States (to Native Indians), Japan

Successful Missions: Korea

Who practiced contextualization? Jesus and the Apostle Paul, and the pharisees did not like that.

Patrick to the Irish, and church leaders did not like that.

> **Group Reflections.**
> 1. How about you? Are you like Jesus and Paul? Or are you like the pharisees?
> 2. What do you think would be the stance of modern-day churches? Explain your rationale.

Business as a Mission

- This begins right where you are before you head out elsewhere.
- Apostle Paul supported himself financially, and all who are called to the marketplace are too a tentmaker.
- See advantages and problems of tentmaking on page 98 and 99.
    - Key advantage is entry to share the gospel with self-sustenance.
    - Key disadvantage is the divided focuses that may prevent sharing of the gospel

Group Reflections.
1. What are the pros and cons of being a tentmaker? What would you personally prefer and why?
2. How can the Church support tentmakers? Discuss implications.

Theology of Contextualization

- Need to understand God in a way that fits their lifestyle
    - For example: do we always pour water on the head for baptism when pouring of water on the person's head is a curse for infertility?
    - Must we all sing Chris Tomlin songs with a guitar and a band?

> 66 Theology needed today is that which is truly Scriptural, completely Christian, and totally relevant. (p. 101)
>
> 66 The message must be understandable to people and must be kept relevant, speaking to the current problems, longings, and ethos of contemporary culture. (p. 102)
>
> 66 Contextualization is not done by specially trained theologians, nor is it done by church leadership alone; instead, everyone must be included in creating the unified theology. (p. 103)
>
> 66 Correct theology is about living it out and bringing our lives to God together in community just as we are. (p. 106)

Group Reflections.
How do you or your church contextualize with others? What would you do to improve this?

Development of Interest-based Small Groups

> ❝ *A small group is self-directed and consists of three or more similar Christians in proximity to each other who personally seek to grow closer to Christ and are willing to share their lives together. (p. 107)*
>
> ❝ *Small groups have the ability to jointly expect and attempt great things for God. (p. 109)*

Group Reflections.
As a person in a leadership role in your local church, how receptive would you be of your church members joining small groups outside your church? Would you promote or discourage it? And how would you support or discourage it?

Chapter Reflections
1. How are you *all things to all people* for the sake of winning them to Christ?
2. Patrick was an effective missionary to the Irish because he knew their culture and language. To whom would you have an effective ministry based on the context God has given you?
3. How do you believe that God has prepared you to fulfill His great calling for your life?

Chapter 6. Our Highest Calling is Love

God called us to relationships, but the church is not known for relationships.

Recap of Chapter 2 – the Gospel, Where the Purpose is to Restore the Relationship with God

- Relationships are the reason why He created Adam and Eve
- Relationships are why God came down in form of a man to die for our sins
- Relationships are why He sent us His Spirit to dwell amongst us

Yet, the Church is not known for relationships. Rather, it is known as a place of ritual and appeasing an angry God to people who did not grow up in a church environment.

Relationships are hard concepts for this generation to understand, and that is why the church is projected to be about activities rather than a relationship. Consider:

- Younger generation (Generation Z) has many distractions that prevent them from knowing how a relationship works
- Millennials/Gen X/Gen Y are often busy and are accustomed to online/social Facebook-like lifestyle, where only positive news are portrayed while keeping any negative inside. As a result, relationships are shallow or non-existent, and they have very few examples of strong relationships to model.
    - Busy parents also lead to children who sees relationships as less meaningful
    - High divorce rates (around 50%) also show children that relationships are less meaningful

Yet, a relationship with God cannot occur when people do not have a framework as to what a relationship looks like. We cannot love God when we are unable to love others.

Dear friends, let us continue to love one another, for love comes from God. Anyone who loves is a child of God and knows God. But anyone who does not love does not know God, for God is love.

1John 4:7-8 (NLT)

Modern Day Small Groups That Do Not Practice Relationships

- Often gather for reasons other than for building relationships. Often, it is centered around worship (no interaction with others) or Bible study (knowledge increase, often taught by one person or a few people).
- People do not know what is going on in the lives of other people. Surface-level relationships.
- As a result, they only share shallow prayer requests and rarely see God involved

> 66 "This is the reason why the Church lacks power and is not known for love, unity, relationships, or community today" (p. 115)

A True Small Group Supports One Another to Look Up Together

> 66 "A true small group is a group of people in relationship with one another, supporting one another to remain in relationship with God together." (p. 116)

- Through their relationship with one another, they can see and value their relationship with God
- They show up even when there is nothing new to talk about
- They continue to talk separately outside the bigger group for lunch and to catch up

Sharing Lives is the Priority of Small Groups.

Unfortunately, when a person begins to have an interest in God, to see if He can help them in their lives' struggles, Christians are often not available.

> ❝ *An unchurched person coming to these one-way conversations, may not receive the relationship, love, and/or answers to the questions they may be experiencing. (p. 119)*

Group Reflections.
1. Do you think of the Church as a place of deep relationships? Would others who do not know Jesus recognize the Church to be a place of relationships? Why or why not? How can we improve this?
2. How can small groups begin to have deep meaningful prayers, and conversation over topics that matter and affect the individuals the most?
3. Are you able to picture what a true small group looks like? Consider Jesus and His disciples doing "discipleship" together. Does it draw the same picture of what we do today in small group gatherings?
4. How can your small group be available when a person becomes interested in knowing about God?

Our Highest Calling (2 Peter 1:5-9)

> **66** *It is this idol of busyness that prevents people from being available for each other, or available to God. (p. 121)*

Faith → Moral Excellence → Knowledge → Self-Control → Patience, Long Suffering → Godliness → Brotherly Love → Love

1. Faith

A starting point and a foundation, but the goal is unshakable/unwavering faith.

Reasons why a Christian must grow beyond this:
- Can be easily misdirected – the "universe" owes them something
- Satan also believes in God
- Faith is fickle – e.g. Praises during the Triumphal Entry vs. "Crucify Him," Peter's denial, and crowds deserting Jesus when Jesus tells them what needs to be done

2. Moral Excellence

Christians represent God by the way they live. They are called to be holy, or be different from the rest of the world.

Reasons why a Christian must grow beyond this:
- Living a good life does not make a person a Christian.
- Scripture clearly says attempts to live a perfect life only shows us that we fall short (Romans 3:19-25)

3. Knowledge

We come to know God more as we study the Scriptures and gain understanding. Christians must be knowledgeable about God and why they believe in what they do.

> Reasons why a Christian must grow beyond this:
> - Knowledge by itself, without love, only leads to pride (1 Corinthians 8:1)
> - Knowledge is for the head, but God calls us to the heart

4. Self-Control

Christians need self-discipline to pray when things get busy or hectic. Christians need self-discipline to praise God, perhaps even in a song, when things get caught in a bind. Self-discipline enables the Christian to believe through the tough times, live their lives with moral excellence when others may sway, and be knowledgeable by continuing to study and meditate on the Scriptures despite many distractions around them.

> Reasons why a Christian must grow beyond this:
> - The purpose of self-discipline is not for oneself, but to love others (1 Corinthians 9:19-27)
> - One may begin to believe they are faithful, live a moral life, and are knowledgeable as long as they continue to be self-disciplined. Heart needs to develop, not the head or self-restraint.

5. Patience

Bear the weight of others over time. Love does not occur in an instant.

> Reasons why a Christian must grow beyond this:
> - Patience needs to be coupled with godliness and love to persist over time.

6. Godliness

Christians must live out a holy and differentiated life

> Reasons why a Christian must grow beyond this:
> - May become religious, perhaps settling at the head level. May become for a show, not from the heart. Love for God and others must lead acts of godliness.

7. **Brotherly Love**
Christians must have the heart of love that is found amongst brothers that have grown up together; a deep friendship

> Reasons why a Christian must grow beyond this:
> - It is an imperfect love, which may be conditional or dependent on circumstances

8. **Agape, Unconditional Love**
   - Christians ought to love as God loves, unconditionally, but it is not possible with human limitation and vacillation of the heart
   - Only God can transform our hearts so that we may love Him and others perfectly. We need God to transform our hearts so that we may stay aligned to His heart and plans.

Many so-called Christians do not strive toward growth and settle at a lower level thinking they have a defensible position if they were to be questioned by God. This direction toward growth is the narrow road (Matthew 7:14).

An example of someone who settled was Abraham's father, Terah. He settled on his way to Canaan. When Terah failed to complete his calling, God gave the call to another, to Terah's son Abram. (Genesis 11-12).

> **Group Reflections.**
> 1. Have you settled at any of the lower levels? Discuss what these levels mean to you and how it may be easy to settle. Also discuss how easy or difficult the journey toward the highest calling may be.
> 2. In the church that you attend, have they settled at a lower level? If you were the key-decision maker at your church, what would you change so that all congregation members may go after the highest calling?
> 3. In your own heart, is love your highest calling? What prevents you from doing that? How can you pursue the highest calling and live differently than the rest of the world?

God is Love (1John 4:7-8)

> ❝ "The One who calls us His children is Love Himself. We are called children of God because of His love in us. Our highest calling is love, and those who do not love do not know God." (p. 138, Chapter 6)

- Matthew 7:21–23 – "I never knew you" – those those who did not do the will of the Father
- Greatest Commandment (Matthew 22:37-40) – Love God and others
- John 13:35 – people know we are followers of Jesus by our love
- Key points of 1John 4:7-8
    - Love amongst Christians shows to the outside world. If we do not love one another, how can we welcome and love anyone who is joining us for the first time?
    - We are given to one another so that we may learn and experience what a relationship is like. That relationship gets projected to God. When we do not have relationship with one another, we cannot have a relationship with God. That's why Jesus teaches us to reconcile relationships before coming to God (Matthew 5:23-24).

Group Reflections.
1. "I never knew you" (See Matthew 7:23) is a message that Christians often assume is not for them. Under what conditions can this message be said to you? What would you change to be one of the people who "actually did the will of the Father" (verse 21) and met "God's laws" (verse 23)?
2. Is there love amongst Christians in your opinion? How or how not? Would people who come to your church for the first time say the same? What would you change if this was not the case?
3. What does a healthy relationship look like? Does this reflect your relationships with others? Does this reflect your relationship with God? How or how not?

Love in Practice (1Corinthians 13)

The three things Christians think highly of in Christian faith.
- Knowledge
- Spiritual gifts
- Service

Yet none of these have any meaning if love was not the purpose (v. 1-3).

Love is
1. Patient: suffering over long time. Even over the difficulties of others.

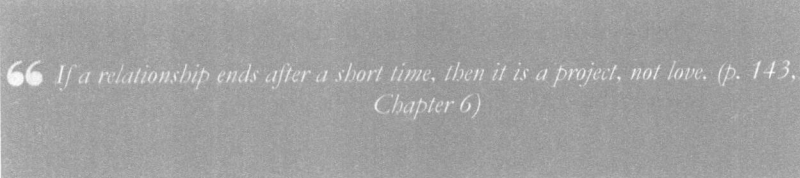

If a relationship ends after a short time, then it is a project, not love. (p. 143, Chapter 6)

2. Kind: to give something when the other person does not deserve it
3. Not jealous, boastful, or proud – our desire to be God:
     i. Jealousy makes something else into a god. It disowns our true God and stops loving others. Examples: Cain kills brother, Sarah dismisses Hagar, King Saul going after David
     b. Boasting and Pride – A person may become proud when well and turn away from God. History of Israel as example
4. Not rude and does not demand its own way
     a. Not being rude refers to doing things to make the person feel comfortable, to nurture the relationship
     b. Does not seek self, but seeks the better for the other person
5. Not irritable and keeps no record of being wronged
     a. Not irritable = not offended by the response from those whom we love
     b. Does not calculate (logic) of wrongs – includes past, and judgment of the present based on past data about the person.
6. Does not rejoice about injustice, rejoices whenever the truth wins out
     a. Celebration of the good and the truth
     b. Does not celebrate over sin or injustice
          i. Both require knowledge – Reflections on Scriptures and Conversations with God is required to fulfill this part of love
7. Never gives up or loses faith, always hopeful, and endures through every circumstance
     a. Always believes in the best for someone, that God can do mighty things through that person. This is why we bless others in prayers trusting that God would do the best for the person

    b. Always hopes
    c. Always bears and endures over time – time factor is mentioned again and *over every circumstance*

Prophecies and speaking in tongues will fade, but love will last forever (1Corinthians 13:8)

Though faith, hope, and love remain, but love is the greatest (1Corinthians 13:13)

Group Reflections.
1. Which aspect of love do you find to be the hardest and why?
2. How does this definition of love toward others affect your love toward God?

Chapter Reflections.
1. What are the callings God has shared with you, and where do you stand in terms of action and faith on what God has planned for you?
2. How can you fulfill the highest calling from where you are today?
3. Which aspects of love would you like to improve upon, and toward whom?

Chapter 7. Being a Disciple to Make Disciples
Small Groups in Practice

Small Groups Have Two-Fold Purpose

1. For the discipleship and growth of Christians, which is done through a rich relationship with one another.
2. To welcome people who are interested in God into the midst of such loving relationships.

Basic Structures of a Small Group

1. Individual Commitment to Growth and Lifesharing, and visits by guests too
    a. Small groups must begin with at least 3 people who have the personal desire to grow and are willing to draw closer to God together through sharing of lives.
    b. Once Christians establish their group, they may welcome other Christians who are similar to them, and perhaps even reach out to people who are similar to them but do not believe in Jesus yet.
2. Proximity and Meeting in Person
    a. The Church gathers often, and this is encouraged by close proximity
    b. Be careful of modern keywords that may negatively impact life-sharing or discipleship
        i. Privacy – we must keep secrets to ourselves and thereby limit sharing of lives.
        ii. Globalization – minimize the need for proximity and meet virtually
    c. Pandemic affects how we meet today – as the Church, we need to consider that and find a solution to enable the ability to share lives together
3. Similarity in Lifestyle and Pursuit
    a. For the purpose of sharing of lives and pursuit.
    b. For contextualization and to welcome people similar to them
    c. Does this divide the Church? No. It welcomes stronger relationships and enables groups to mingle when desired.
4. Frequent Meetings over time
    a. Weekly meetings
    b. Meetings outside, especially in each other's homes, work, and other places to welcome others into each other's lives

Results of Each Gathering

- Nothing: but the members know that is ok. Simply do as originally planned and trust God for the long-lasting results.
- Something: Allow something else to occur beyond regular planning. Such as one of the members coming with a problem or a question in their mind for the members to engage in together through dialogue and prayer.
- Everything: From even regular plans, God may bring about a great fear about a certain sin, or something that the members ought to pray for. God may bring about life transformations over time especially as breakthroughs, healings, and miracles come about. God may bring about new direction and a new heart.

Components of a Small Group (Acts 2:42)

- Study / devotion to the Word of God
- Fellowship, or spending unrushed time together
- Eating together
- Prayer

Meeting Location

- A place where unrushed fellowship can occur. Preferably a place where one shares lives, such as homes or personal office spaces.

Characteristics of Strong Small Groups

- Self-directed
- Frequent Communication between members
- Daily Bible readings and sharing a favorite verse
- Coordinator or leader that serves the group
- Small group size – consistently under 8
- Welcome variations – allow for changes, and go out and have a nice meal together
- Meet weekly
- Same Gender
- A place to come and see – welcoming new members

Possible Content for Small Group Meetings

- Remember, content is not the focus! Possible "backup" materials:
  - Our Daily Bread, Monday Manna, Scripture reading and sharing
  - Topics of interest - such as fatherhood, representing Christ in the marketplace, etc.
- Go back to Acts 2:42 and mix and match. Remember, not all four needs to be held at every meeting.

Eat Together! (Eating Ministry)

- It says that we are all the same. Pastors to non-pastors, executives to assistants, people of all races and genders. We attribute our thanks to God and do what we all do, which is eat. We can share lives together as we do.

Power Evangelism

- Yes. Let there be healings, miracles, and breakthroughs in circumstances, but within the context of loving relationships. Build the discipleship (relationships) over time, yet let God take over when He directs you to do so.

Proper Length of Small Group Meetings

- Anything that is unrushed. Seems open-ended meetings do best.

Special Small Group – Families

- Fathers, if not, mothers, ought to lead their families in frequent small group meetings.
    - Provides and teaches the goal of a loving community
    - Children can grow modeling their parents

Number of Small Groups to Join

- One, but with caveats. The ability to share lives is how you determine that number.

When Should I Start a Small Group?

- When three or more Christians willing to commit to growth together

When Should We Disband?

- When two people are consistently meeting together. Just join another small group together to continue the fellowship.

When and How Should We Split?

- When there are 9 or more people consistently gathering
- Still remain in contact with releasing small group, and perhaps even hold joint gatherings along the way

What a Small Group is Not

- A mass or a group that extends to more than twelve (12) people consistently
- A worship service
- A place for sermons by the educated (or positional) few
- A one person show
- Established as an extension of administrative church work
- Always associated with a local church

How to Evangelize

- Make disciples. Welcome others to your loving group.

Role of Pastors in Small Groups

- Be available
- Welcome dialogue and encourage dialogue
- Enable Christians under their care to minister, that is, to share the Scriptures, pray for one another, visit others in need, and hold deep relationships with one another.

Goal of Every Meeting

- Bring our lives and pursuits together to Jesus. This occurs through the sharing of lives.
    - Trust God together that He would provide supernaturally for His great calling

Chapter Reflections.
1. What are some changes, if any, that you would make to your small-group meetings? How would you explain the rationale for those changes?
2. What are some actions you may need to incorporate in order to receive prayer requests from others that are deep, personal, and important (compared to shallow, impersonal requests)?

Do you have experiences in small groups that may be helpful?

Do you have any questions or want to hear other people's views on small group development?

Support development of small groups by sharing your views or ask your questions at:

www.ourhighestcalling.com

More books by Prayer Tents Media

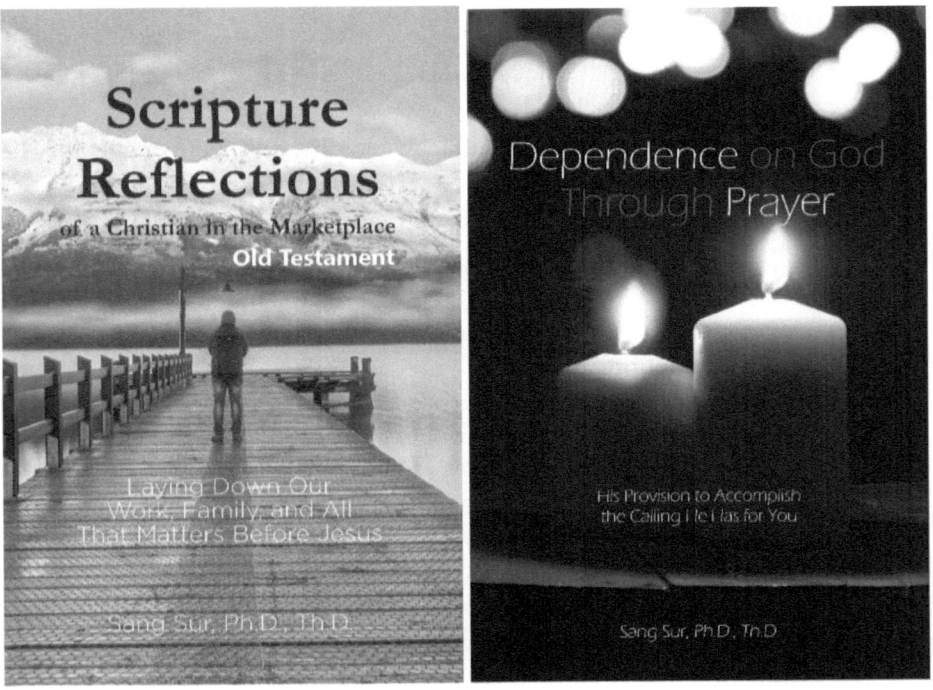

Find more at **www.prayertents.com/store**

www.ingramcontent.com/pod-product-compliance
Lightning Source LLC
Chambersburg PA
CBHW021452070526
44577CB00002B/378